International Labour Office

WORKPLACE COOPERATION:

An introductory guide

Robert Heron
David Macdonald
Caroline Vandenabeele

ILO East Asia Multidisciplinary Advisory Team
ILO Regional Office for Asia and the Pacific
Bangkok

First published 1997

ISBN 92-2-110876-7

ILO publications can be obtained through major booksellers or ILO local offices in many countries, or direct from Customer Service, ILO Publications, International Labour Office, CH-1211 Geneva 22, Switzerland. A catalogue or list of new publications will be sent free of charge from the above address.

Printed in Thailand

Foreword

Many enterprises are endeavouring to improve their performance to meet the challenge of increased competition in domestic and world markets. They are realizing that their own employees – workers as well as managers – can and should be better involved and utilized. These enterprises have seen what others have achieved: investing in strategies to improve workplace relations through cooperative means (e.g. by information sharing, consultation and two-way communication) can promote innovation, improve flexibility and facilitate change. It can increase enterprise productivity, efficiency and competitiveness, and lead to more job satisfaction and better wages and working conditions for workers. It should also reduce the incidence of industrial disputes.

This publication outlines what workplace cooperation is, the principles and preconditions which underpin it, its objectives, who are involved, the forms such cooperation may take, and the factors which will influence its development.

There is, however, no single blueprint or model for workplace cooperation since each enterprise is different. The particular strategy adopted by an enterprise must take into account its size, whether it is at one location or geographically dispersed, the composition of its workforce, its industrial relations history and other related matters. Existing industrial relations arrangements in the enterprise (more importantly, collective bargaining processes and issues dealt with in that context) must be considered. Influences external to the enterprise – the political environment, the economic system, the industrial relations legislative and institutional framework, and custom and practice – will also have to be borne in mind.

Improving workplace relations requires sustained commitment by managers, workers and their representatives if positive and lasting changes are to be secured. This will take time and effort, but the benefits to all can be considerable.

The guide has been prepared by Mr Robert Heron, Senior Labour Administration Specialist, Mr David Macdonald, Senior Industrial Relations Specialist, and Ms Caroline Vandenabeele, Associate Expert on Labour Law and Industrial Relations, of the ILO East Asia Multidisciplinary Advisory Team.

Translation of the guide into national languages is encouraged. Users' comments and suggestions for its improvement are appreciated.

W.R. Simpson
Director
ILO East Asia Multidisciplinary
Advisory Team (ILO/EASMAT)

Bangkok
October 1997

Table of contents

1 What is workplace cooperation?

A. Definitions

Workplace cooperation can mean:

- workers' participation or involvement in decision-making
- labour-management cooperation
- participative or cooperative practices in an enterprise.

Workplace cooperation can take various forms, such as information sharing, direct or indirect consultation, and financial participation. Collective bargaining is also a form of and a vehicle for workplace cooperation (see chapter 3).

Workplace cooperation is a process whereby workers or their representatives participate with management, through consultation and discussion, in resolving issues of common concern.

Workplace cooperation is essentially a bipartite process, between management and workers, in which the role of the third party, the government, is confined to a promotional and facilitative one.

> In workplace cooperation, managers and workers in an enterprise come together to talk and listen to each other in order to find mutually acceptable ways of dealing with common problems and issues.

B. Who are involved?

The key players in workplace cooperation are managers and workers in enterprises.

Which particular **managers and workers** are involved will depend on the issue to be addressed.

Examples:

In workplace cooperation related to improving machine safety, the workers operating the machines, the supervisor concerned as well as a safety engineer should be involved.

In the case of financial participation, the financial manager should be involved.

In unionized enterprises, **union representatives** – who form an existing channel for communication between management and workers – should be involved. Workplace cooperation, however, is not limited to communication with and through union representatives, but concerns all workers in the workplace, whether unionized or not.

Employers' and workers' organizations outside the enterprise have an important role in promoting the concept of workplace cooperation among their members and providing them with advice, education and training.

The **government's** role is confined to promoting and facilitating workplace cooperation by:

- working with employers' and workers' organizations to develop a national policy and strategy or plan of action as a framework for workplace cooperation
- providing information and facilitative materials (e.g. practical guidelines)
- promoting and disseminating 'best practice' models

2 What are the objectives of workplace cooperation?

Developing more cooperative working relations in the enterprise can contribute to:

- increased efficiency, productivity and competitiveness of the enterprise

  Example:

  In a manufacturing enterprise, discussion with shop-floor workers would be useful to identify existing weaknesses in the assembly line (e.g. organization of the process, quality of goods produced) before introducing new technology in order to raise efficiency and productivity.

- better enterprise industrial relations

  Example:

  If workers know that management is seriously interested in discussing workplace issues, the occurrence of industrial disputes and related actions will be reduced.

- an improved working environment

  Example:

  Workers and front-line supervisors know best what is hazardous on the shop floor and why the hazards exist. They should be consulted on ways and means of improving the situation.

- increased job satisfaction and effectiveness

  Example:

  Training and skill development will have a greater impact if workers are consulted on the kind of training they need to enhance job satisfaction and effectiveness. This is particularly important when:

  - introducing new technology
  - improving product and service quality
  - introducing new products or services
  - restructuring the enterprise

- more effective decision-making within the enterprise

  Example:

  If an enterprise seeks to change its shift system, it would be a good practice to inform workers of the reasons for the change. It would also be useful to consult workers on the feasibility of the change and the possible problems that may arise. If workers can understand the reasons for the change and feel that their opinions have been taken into consideration, the new shift system is likely to be implemented more smoothly.

- more equitable sharing of enterprise profits by workers

  Example:

  Discussions between management and workers can help clarify what methods will be used to calculate workers' share of profits, instead of their share being unilaterally determined by management.

People who have been informed
why something is happening,
and have been consulted on
how it should happen,
will be much more willing
to **make** it happen.

3 Forms of workers' participation

A. Information sharing

Information sharing is the regular and systematic provision, by management to workers, of accurate and comprehensive information on a range of personnel, financial, production, developmental and organizational matters.

Information sharing:

- informs workers about what is happening and why
- serves as a prerequisite for other forms of workplace cooperation

  Example:

  Management wishes to have initial discussions with workers or their representatives on the feasibility of wage increases or on changes in the wage system. To ensure a balanced and constructive discussion, it is necessary to share information on the financial situation and future prospects of the enterprise in a transparent way.

Information sharing can take place through various means, including:

- mass meetings
- meetings with representatives of different sections of the enterprise

- noticeboards
- in-house newsletters or journals
- individual discussions

B. Consultation

Consultation is a process by which management seeks the views of workers on certain issues, but retains the power to make decisions on them.

Consultation can be direct or indirect.

1. Direct consultation

In direct consultation, management solicits the views of workers without the involvement of any intermediary. This can be done through:

- questionnaires
- suggestion boxes
- discussions with individual workers or small groups of workers

Direct consultation focuses mainly on day-to-day issues concerning the immediate work situation and the job content. It is especially useful when considering issues such as:

- overtime schedules
- occupational safety and health
- changes to job design and work organization
- plant or workplace layout
- training and skill development

2. Indirect consultation

Consultation can also be indirect, through the involvement of a formally constituted body.

The consultative body (e.g. a committee representative of both workers' and employers' interests) is established to discuss matters of mutual concern.

The issues to be considered when setting up a consultative body include the following:

- What is the range of issues that will be open to consultation and who will decide on this?
- How are workers' representatives chosen? Will they be elected or selected?
- What is the role of trade unions?

Indirect consultation is directed at broader, longer-term issues related to:

- personnel policy and practices
- workers' amenities
- introducing new technology
- improving market performance
- plant reorganization (including closure)

> Consultation can only be effective
> if workers are properly informed
> on the issue on which their views are sought.

In some cases the consultative body can have more responsibility than mere consultation. It can be a forum where workers' and employers' representatives come together to consider and **take decisions** on matters of common interest.

There can only be real **joint decision-making**:

- if the decisions are made unanimously, or
- where decisions are taken by voting, there is equal representation of workers and managers.

C. Collective bargaining

Collective bargaining at the enterprise level is the process by which the employer and representatives of workers voluntarily discuss and negotiate mutually acceptable terms and conditions of employment which are valid for a given period of time.

Collective bargaining is both:

- a form of workplace cooperation
- a vehicle for workplace cooperation

It is **a form of workplace cooperation** because it provides a clear means by which issues of common concern to managers, workers and trade unions can be resolved.

There are some fundamental **differences between collective bargaining** (in its traditional form) **and workplace cooperation.**

- Collective bargaining normally takes place at fixed intervals (annually or biennially) whereas workplace cooperation is a continuing process.
- Collective bargaining can occur at the national, industry or enterprise level. Workplace cooperation is exclusively an enterprise-level activity and can take place in one particular work unit.
- The agreements reached in collective bargaining are usually legally binding. Decisions resulting from workplace consultative mechanisms are advisory to management, but not legally binding.
- Collective bargaining traditionally involves issues which are more conflictual in nature, such as wages and conditions of employment. Workplace cooperation covers a much broader range of subjects.

- Collective bargaining usually takes place through trade unions. In workplace cooperation the representative of workers need not be a trade unionist, but can be a person or body elected or appointed to represent workers, including non-unionized workers.

In many countries collective bargaining is now changing in so far as:

- it is involving negotiations over a broader range of issues (including workplace cooperation)
- it has become a more permanent problem-solving mechanism
- it has become less conflictual and confrontational

Collective bargaining is also **a vehicle for workplace cooperation** in that it can ensure, by mutual agreement, that participative practices are integrated into the day-to-day operations of the enterprise.

Examples:

Through collective bargaining it can be agreed that new technology will not be introduced unless the workers concerned have been extensively consulted on such matters as the kind of technology required, the need for retraining and the overall impact on employment in their unit.

Joint consultation committees can be provided for under collective agreements, specifying such elements as the number of representatives, the frequency with which such committees will meet and the issues which can be discussed.

Both collective bargaining and workplace cooperation **aim** at giving workers a say in decisions which affect them.

D. Self-managed work groups

Workplace cooperation can result in the setting up of teams or groups of workers (usually six to ten persons) who have considerable autonomy for their own operations.

The degree of **autonomy of the work group** can vary widely, but there is usually relative freedom from close supervision and external controls. Autonomy can relate to:

- decisions on work targets
- the way group tasks are allocated and carried out
- acceptance and allocation of additional work
- working hours (e.g. when to have meal breaks and the basis for overtime allocation)
- leadership of the group

The **role of the supervisor** of the work group becomes one of planning, training and developing group members, and facilitating relations with other areas of the enterprise.

In general, each work group is responsible for a specific product or service, enabling members to undertake a variety of roles or tasks.

The effectiveness of a semi-autonomous work group will be maximized if:

- it is responsible for the full range of activities to complete a given task
- it regulates its work within agreed and understood guidelines
- it has all the skills needed to carry out the task

- it has clear criteria for performance and remuneration
- it has detailed and regular feedback on its objectives, quality standards and performance
- its size and structure facilitates good communication
- it has the necessary materials and equipment as well as effective support services

Self-managed work groups
aim at
building group cohesion,
giving workers more responsibility
and increasing job satisfaction.

E. Financial participation

Theoretically, financial participation is a form of workers' participation in the ownership, policy formulation, management or financial results of the enterprise.

Example:

Through the holding of shares, workers - like other shareholders - can be involved in policy development of the enterprise by participating in meetings shareholders are entitled to attend.

In reality, financial participation is often no more than a sharing in the outputs of the enterprise rather than in decisions concerning inputs and processes.

Example:

Participation in management of the enterprise through the holding of shares would only be possible if the workers owned sufficient shares to influence decisions at the annual meeting.

Financial participation by workers, in itself, is not sufficient to ensure improved workplace cooperation. It should be integrated with, support and complement other forms of workers' participation.

Through **financial information sharing** workers are informed about the financial situation of the enterprise. Financial information sharing is essential for financial participation and other forms of workplace cooperation.

Example:

Management wants to consult with workers about restructuring the enterprise which will involve important investment decisions. Consultation can only be useful if workers know the financial situation of the enterprise.

The main forms of financial participation are:

- payment-by-results schemes (i.e. bonus and piece-work payments)
- profit-sharing schemes
- productivity-sharing schemes
- employee share-ownership (i.e. share/stock acquisition) schemes

In **payment-by-results schemes** the pay of the worker is linked with his or her output or with the output of his or her work group.

In **profit-sharing schemes** the worker receives his or her normal remuneration, as well as an additional amount based on the profits of the enterprise. The additional amount can be based on:

- a predetermined percentage of profit. In this case, the profit is paid before shareholders get their dividends
- the declared dividends payable to shareholders, whether the shareholders are outsiders or workers

Questions to be asked prior to the establishment of profit-sharing schemes include the following:

- What will be the basis for calculation of profit?
- How often will payments be made?
- Will payment be made on a year-to-year basis or be deferred to a later date, such as on retirement?
- Which types of workers are eligible to participate in the scheme?

In **productivity-sharing schemes** the worker receives his or her normal remuneration plus an amount based on some measure of labour productivity **before** profit is calculated. It is different from payment-by-results schemes. In the case of the latter the total amount of remuneration received depends on the actual outputs, without guaranteed basic remuneration, unless, of course, minimum wage laws apply.

Issues to consider in establishing productivity-sharing schemes include the following:

- How will productivity increases be measured?
- How frequently will payments be made and to whom?
- Will the scheme be used to reduce existing levels of remuneration?
- How will the scheme be monitored?

In **employee share-ownership schemes** employees share in enterprise profits through dividends.

Employee share-ownership schemes can operate on a direct or indirect basis.

- On a direct basis, shares are owned by individual employees.
- Under indirect ownership, the shares are owned by the employees as a group, e.g. a pension fund can buy shares in the enterprise on behalf of all employees.

Shares bought by workers under employee share-ownership schemes, may differ from the company's shares listed on the stock market in:

- price
- conditions under which they can be bought and sold
- voting rights

Workplace cooperation is a **means** of consulting and deciding on financial participation, rather than financial participation being a **form** of active workplace cooperation.

What are the external influences?

Workplace cooperation does not take place in a vacuum. Several environmental factors influence the way it is introduced, regulated and developed, and the forms it takes.

A. International labour standards

There are various international instruments related to workers' participation in the enterprise. Primarily, these take the form of international labour Recommendations adopted by the International Labour Organization.

These Recommendations promote and provide guidelines for effective consultative and cooperative practices between employers, workers and trade unions at the enterprise, industry and national levels. They emphasize that the consultative and cooperative practices they advocate should not be a substitute for collective bargaining.

It is important to note that Recommendations have no legal status and provide advice to guide national policy and practice. Conventions, by contrast, create legal obligations once they are ratified by an ILO member State.

The relevant ILO instruments are the:

- Workers' Representatives Convention, 1971 (No. 135)
- Cooperation at the Level of the Undertaking Recommendation, 1952 (No. 94)

- Consultation (Industrial and National Levels) Recommendation, 1960 (No. 113)
- Communications within the Undertaking Recommendation, 1967 (No. 129)
- Examination of Grievances Recommendation, 1967 (No. 130)

The full text of each of these instruments is included in the annex.

B. National factors

The framework in which workplace cooperation takes place varies from country to country. It can depend on a country's culture and traditions and will also be influenced by its industrial relations history.

> Example:
>
> In a country where, traditionally, detailed legislation has been the prime source for guiding the development of industrial relations, the framework for workers' participation might also be set out through legislation. On the other hand, in a country where collective bargaining has had a significant role, workers' participation may be more easily introduced through collective bargaining.

Legislation as a framework for introducing workers' participation can be facilitative or prescriptive.

> Example:
>
> In some countries there is a legal obligation for enterprises employing over 50 workers to establish enterprise committees and/or occupational safety and health councils. This is a form of prescriptive legislation. Facilitative legislation, by contrast, might set out various principles and identify forms of workers' participation as a guide to employers and workers, without specifying a particular approach.

Collective bargaining can be used as the vehicle for introducing workplace cooperation. This can occur through enterprise-, industry- or national-level bargaining. Collective agreements at the national and industry levels can set out the **framework** for workplace cooperation. But the **details** (e.g. the forms of participation, the particular issues, who are involved) will need to be identified and addressed at the enterprise level.

Workplace cooperation introduced through collective bargaining can be general or linked to the subject matter of a specific collective agreement.

> Example:
>
> An enterprise wishes to introduce new technology. Agreement is reached through collective bargaining that workers will not be made redundant as a result of the introduction of this technology. The agreement also specifies that consultation will take place with the workers likely to be affected if the introduction of further technology is planned.

In many countries workplace cooperation is introduced through **voluntary agreements** between employers, workers and their representatives.

> Workers' participation
> can be regulated by law
> or collective agreements,
> but the parties need to be **willing**
> to consult and cooperate
> if it is to be successful.

C. Cultural factors

The cultural factors that may influence workplace cooperation can be national, local or relate directly to corporate culture.

Examples:

It may be easier to introduce workplace cooperation in group-oriented cultures than in individual-oriented cultures.

Cultures that have hierarchical structures may find it more difficult to introduce workers' participation.

The **culture and history of the enterprise** will have an important influence on the development of workplace cooperation.

Example:

Workplace cooperation will be more difficult to develop in enterprises having a poor industrial relations record and conflictual relations between workers and management. The first requirement here will be to build up trust and confidence between all parties.

Other factors related to the enterprise which will have an influence on workplace cooperation include:

- the size and structure of the enterprise

Examples:

In an enterprise with less than 50 workers, direct forms of workers' participation are feasible. In an enterprise having over 100 workers, it will be better to introduce indirect forms of participation.

In a geographically dispersed enterprise the involvement of workers in decision-making will be more effective if it is organized on a decentralized basis.

- the degree of functional and organizational diversity within the enterprise

  Example:

  Workers in a manufacturing enterprise which has personnel, planning and marketing divisions, as well as an assembly line, are likely to be subject to different pay systems. Introducing financial participation will need careful thought, taking into account the differences in work between all areas of the enterprise.

- managerial style

  Example:

  It will be more difficult to establish a consultative body in an enterprise where the manager has traditionally had an autocratic approach to directing, controlling and taking decisions than in an enterprises where the role of the manager is one of adviser, facilitator and provider of support.

- existing working arrangements and the composition of the workforce

  Example:

  In establishing a consultative body in an enterprise having a shift system, it will be necessary to ensure that all workers and supervisors from all shifts are represented.

- work processes and technology

  Example:

  Workers' participation in an enterprise with labour-intensive assembly work will be different from an enterprise with capital-intensive continuous process technologies with a high degree of automation. In the former, financial participation through piece work may be appropriate. In the latter, this form of financial participation is not relevant.

D. Experience of other enterprises

In establishing workplace cooperation, it is useful to take a closer look at what other enterprises have done in this field, what has worked and what has not.

It should be remembered, however, that what works well in one enterprise may not necessarily work well in another.

The **government and workers' and employers' organizations** play an important role in:

- collecting information about workplace cooperation in different enterprises
- comparing and analysing results
- identifying 'best practice' models
- disseminating information

In studying the examples of other enterprises,
focus not only on
what has worked or not worked
but also on
why it did or did not work.

Preconditions for workplace cooperation

Developing greater involvement of workers in resolving day-to-day issues and improving the level of cooperation between workers and managers will have a better chance of success if certain preconditions are met.

Before introducing changes to improve cooperation at the workplace, workers and management need to have a joint understanding and agreement on:

- two-way communication, information sharing, and genuine consultation and participation
- the present situation, and its strengths and weaknesses
- the objectives and strategies for improving cooperation
- how such cooperation will relate to other existing processes in the enterprise which also deal with workplace issues, such as collective bargaining

Other factors which will influence the success of introducing workplace cooperation are mentioned below:

- From the outset all workers should be given the opportunity to be involved in discussing the planned change.
- The focus should be on substantial and well-defined issues, such as improving workplace safety and health.
- There is no single approach for introducing workplace cooperation. The approach to be taken will depend on the particular needs and circumstances of each enterprise.
- More effective cooperation in the workplace cannot be achieved overnight. It requires a long-term perspective and commitment.

Annex

Convention No. 135

Convention concerning Protection and Facilities to be Afforded to Workers' Representatives in the Undertaking [1]

The General Conference of the International Labour Organization,

Having been convened at Geneva by the Governing Body of the International Labour Office, and having met in its Fifty-sixth Session on 2 June 1971, and

Noting the terms of the Right to Organize and Collective Bargaining Convention, 1949, which provides for protection of workers against acts of anti-union discrimination in respect of their employment, and

Considering that it is desirable to supplement these terms with respect to workers' representatives, and

Having decided upon the adoption of certain proposals with regard to protection and facilities afforded to workers' representatives in the undertaking, which is the fifth item on the agenda of the session, and

Having determined that these proposals shall take the form of an international Convention,

adopts this twenty-third day of June of the year one thousand nine hundred and seventy-one, the following Convention, which may be cited as the Workers' Representatives Convention, 1971:

---

[1] Date of coming into force: 30 June 1973

Article 1

Workers' representatives in the undertaking shall enjoy effective protection against any act prejudicial to them, including dismissal, based on their status or activities as a workers' representative or on union membership or participation in union activities, in so far as they act in conformity with existing laws or collective agreements or other jointly agreed arrangements.

Article 2

1. Such facilities in the undertaking shall be afforded to workers' representatives as may be appropriate in order to enable them to carry out their functions promptly and efficiently.

2. In this connection account shall be taken of the characteristics of the industrial relations system of the country and the needs, size and capabilities of the undertaking concerned.

3. The granting of such facilities shall not impair the efficient operation of the undertaking concerned.

Article 3

For the purpose of this Convention the term "workers' representatives" means persons who are recognized as such under national law or practice, whether they are –

(a) trade union representatives, namely, representatives designated or elected by trade unions or by members of such unions; or

(b) elected representatives, namely, representatives who are freely elected by the workers of the undertaking in accordance with provisions of national laws or regulations or of collective agreements and whose functions do not include activities which are recognized as the exclusive prerogative of trade unions in the country concerned.

Article 4

National laws or regulations, collective agreements, arbitration awards or court decisions may determine the type or types of workers' representatives which shall be entitled to the protection and facilities provided for in this Convention.

Article 5

Where there exist in the same undertaking both trade union representatives and elected representatives, appropriate measures shall be taken, wherever necessary, to ensure that the existence of elected representatives is not used to undermine the position of the trade unions concerned or their representatives and to encourage cooperation on all relevant matters between the elected representatives and the trade unions concerned and their representatives.

Article 6

Effect may be given to this Convention through national laws or regulations or collective agreements, or in any other manner consistent with national practice.

Recommendation No. 94

Recommendation concerning Consultation and Cooperation between Employers and Workers at the Level of the Undertaking

The General Conference of the International Labour Organization,

Having been convened at Geneva by the Governing Body of the International Labour Office, and having met in its Thirty-fifth Session on 4 June 1952, and

Having decided upon the adoption of certain proposals with regard to consultation and cooperation between employers and workers at the level of the undertaking, which is included in the sixth item on the agenda of the session, and

Having determined that these proposals shall take the form of a Recommendation designed to be implemented by the parties concerned or by the public authorities as may be appropriate under national conditions,

adopts this twenty-sixth day of June of the year one thousand nine hundred and fifty-two, the following Recommendation, which may be cited as the Cooperation at the Level of the Undertaking Recommendation, 1952:

1. Appropriate steps should be taken to promote consultation and cooperation between employers and workers at the level of the undertaking on matters of mutual concern not within the scope of collective bargaining machinery, or not normally dealt with by other machinery concerned with the determination of terms and conditions of employment.

2. In accordance with national custom or practice, such consultation and cooperation should be –

(a) facilitated by the encouragement of voluntary agreements between the parties, or

(b) promoted by laws or regulations which would establish bodies for consultation and cooperation and determine their scope, functions, structure and methods of operation as may be appropriate to the conditions in the various undertakings, or

(c) facilitated or promoted by a combination of these methods.

Recommendation No. 113

Recommendation concerning Consultation and Cooperation between Public Authorities and Employers' and Workers' Organizations at the Industrial and National Levels

The General Conference of the International Labour Organization,

Having been convened at Geneva by the Governing Body of the International Labour Office, and having met in its Forty-fourth Session on 1 June 1960, and

Having decided upon the adoption of certain proposals with regard to consultation and cooperation between public authorities and employers' and workers' organizations at the industrial and national levels, which is the fifth item on the agenda of the session, and

Having determined that these proposals shall take the form of a Recommendation,

adopts this twentieth day of June of the year one thousand nine hundred and sixty, the following Recommendation, which may be cited as the Consultation (Industrial and National Levels) Recommendation, 1960:

1. (1) Measures appropriate to national conditions should be taken to promote effective consultation and cooperation at the industrial and national levels between public authorities and employers' and workers' organizations, as well as between these organizations, for the purposes indicated in Paragraphs 4 and 5 below, and on such other matters of mutual concern as the parties may determine.

(2) Such measures should be applied without discrimination of any kind against these organizations or amongst them on grounds such as the race, sex, religion, political opinion or national extraction of their members.

2. Such consultation and cooperation should not derogate from freedom of association or from the rights of employers' and workers' organizations, including their right of collective bargaining.

3. In accordance with national custom or practice, such consultation and cooperation should be provided for or facilitated –

(a) by voluntary action on the part of the employers' and workers' organizations; or

(b) by promotional action on the part of the public authorities; or

(c) by laws or regulations; or

(d) by a combination of any of these methods.

4. Such consultation and cooperation should have the general objective of promoting mutual understanding and good relations between public authorities and employers' and workers' organizations, as well as between these organizations, with a view to developing the economy as a whole or individual branches thereof, improving conditions of work and raising standards of living.

5. Such consultation and cooperation should aim, in particular–

(a) at joint consideration by employers' and workers' organizations of matters of mutual concern with a view to arriving, to the fullest possible extent, at agreed solutions; and

(b) at ensuring that the competent public authorities seek the views, advice and assistance of employers' and workers' organizations in an appropriate manner, in respect of such matters as –

    (i) the preparation and implementation of laws and regulations affecting their interests;

    (ii) the establishment and functioning of national bodies, such as those responsible for organization of employment, vocational training and retraining, labour protection, industrial health and safety, productivity, social security and welfare; and

    (iii) the elaboration and implementation of plans of economic and social development.

Recommendation No. 129

Recommendation concerning Communications between Management and Workers within the Undertaking

The General Conference of the International Labour Organization,

Having been convened at Geneva by the Governing Body of the International Labour Office, and having met in its Fifty-first Session on 7 June 1967, and

Noting the terms of the Cooperation at the Level of the Undertaking Recommendation, 1952, and

Considering that additional standards are called for, and

Having decided upon the adoption of certain proposals with regard to communications within the undertaking, which is included in the fifth item on the agenda of the session, and

Having determined that these proposals shall take the form of a Recommendation,

adopts this twenty-eighth day of June of the year one thousand nine hundred and sixty-seven, the following Recommendation, which may be cited as the Communications within the Undertaking Recommendation, 1967:

I. General Considerations

1. Each Member should take appropriate action to bring the provisions of this Recommendation to the attention of persons, organizations and authorities who may be concerned with the establishment and application of policies concerning communications between management and workers within undertakings.

2. (1) Employers and their organizations as well as workers and their organizations should, in their common interest, recognize the importance of a climate of mutual understanding and confidence within undertakings that is favourable both to the efficiency of the undertaking and to the aspirations of the workers.

(2) This climate should be promoted by the rapid dissemination and exchange of information, as complete and objective as possible, relating to the various aspects of the life of the undertaking and to the social conditions of the workers.

(3) With a view to the development of such a climate management should, after consultation with workers' representatives, adopt appropriate measures to apply an effective policy of communication with the workers and their representatives.

3. An effective policy of communication should ensure that information is given and that consultation takes place between the parties concerned before decisions on matters of major interest are taken by management, in so far as disclosure of the information will not cause damage to either party.

4. The communication methods should in no way derogate from freedom of association; they should in no way cause prejudice to freely chosen workers' representatives or to their organizations or curtail the functions of bodies representative of the workers in conformity with national law and practice.

5. Employers' and workers' organizations should have mutual consultations and exchanges of views in order to examine the measures to be taken with a view to encouraging and promoting the acceptance of communications policies and their effective application.

6. Steps should be taken to train those concerned in the use of communication methods and to make them, as far as possible, conversant with all the subjects in respect of which communication should take place.

7. In the establishment and application of a communications policy, management, employers' and workers' organizations, bodies representative of the workers and, where appropriate under national conditions, public authorities should be guided by the provisions of Part II below.

II. Elements for a Communications Policy within the Undertaking

8. Any communications policy should be adapted to the nature of the undertaking concerned, account being taken of its size and of the composition and interests of the workforce.

9. With a view to fulfilling its purpose, any communications system within the undertaking should be designed to ensure genuine and regular two-way communication –

(a) between representatives of management (head of the undertaking, department chief, foreman, etc.) and the workers; and

(b) between the head of the undertaking, the director of personnel or any other representative of top management and trade union representatives or such other persons as may, under national law or practice, or under collective agreements, have the task of representing the interests of the workers at the level of the undertaking.

10. Where the management desires to transmit information through workers' representatives, the latter, if they agree to do so, should be given the means to communicate such information rapidly and completely to the workers concerned.

11. Management should, in choosing the channel or channels of communication which it considers appropriate for the type of information to be transmitted, take due account of the difference in the nature of the functions of supervisors and workers' representatives so as not to weaken their respective positions.

12. The selection of the appropriate medium of communication, and its timing, should be on the basis of the circumstances of each particular situation, account being taken of national practice.

13. Media of communication may include –

(a) meetings for the purpose of exchanging views and information;

(b) media aimed at given groups of workers, such as supervisors' bulletins and personnel policy manuals;

(c) mass media such as house journals and magazines; newsletters and information and induction leaflets; noticeboards; annual or financial reports presented in a form understandable to all the workers; employee letters; exhibitions; plant visits; films; filmstrips and slides; radio and television;

(d) media aimed at permitting workers to submit suggestions and to express their ideas on questions relating to the operation of the undertaking.

14. The information to be communicated and its presentation should be determined with a view to mutual understanding in regard to the problems posed by the complexity of the undertaking's activities.

15. (1) The information to be given by management should, account being taken of its nature, be addressed either to the workers' representatives or to the workers and should, as far as possible, include all matters of interest to the workers relating to the operation and future prospects of the undertaking and to the present and future situation of the workers, in so far as disclosure of the information will not cause damage to the parties.

(2) In particular, management should give information regarding–

(a) general conditions of employment, including engagement, transfer and termination of employment;

(b) job descriptions and the place of particular jobs within the structure of the undertaking;

(c) possibilities of training and prospects of advancement within the undertaking;

(d) general working conditions;

(e) occupational safety and health regulations and instructions for the prevention of accidents and occupational diseases;

(f) procedures for the examination of grievances as well as the rules and practices governing their operation and the conditions for having recourse to them;

(g) personnel welfare services (medical care, health, canteens, housing, leisure, savings and banking facilities, etc.);

(h) social security or social assistance schemes in the undertaking;

(i) the regulations of national social security schemes to which the workers are subject by virtue of their employment in the undertaking;

(j) the general situation of the undertaking and prospects or plans for its future development;

(k) the explanation of decisions which are likely to affect directly or indirectly the situation of workers in the undertaking;

(l) methods of consultation and discussion and of cooperation between management and its representatives, on the one hand, and the workers and their representatives on the other.

(3) In the case of a question which has been the subject of negotiations between the employer and the workers or their representatives in the undertaking or of a collective agreement concluded at a level beyond that of the undertaking, the information should make express reference thereto.

Recommendation No. 130

Recommendation concerning the Examination of Grievances within the Enterprise with a View to their Settlement

The General Conference of the International Labour Organization,

Having been convened at Geneva by the Governing Body of the International Labour Office, and having met in its Fifty-first Session on 7 June 1967, and

Noting the terms of existing international labour Recommendations dealing with various aspects of labour-management relations, and in particular the Collective Agreements Recommendation, 1951, the Voluntary Conciliation and Arbitration Recommendation, 1951, the Cooperation at the Level of the Undertaking Recommendation, 1952, and the Termination of Employment Recommendation, 1963, and

Considering that additional standards are called for, and

Noting the terms of the Communications within the Undertaking Recommendation, 1967, and

Having decided upon the adoption of certain proposals with regard to the examination of grievances within the undertaking, which is included in the fifth item on the agenda of the session, and

Having determined that these proposals shall take the form of a Recommendation,

adopts this twenty-ninth day of June of the year one thousand nine hundred and sixty-seven, the following Recommendation, which may be cited as the Examination of Grievances Recommendation, 1967:

I. Methods of Implementation

1. Effect may be given to this Recommendation through national laws or regulations, collective agreements, works rules, or arbitration awards, or in such other manner consistent with national practice as may be appropriate under national conditions.

II. General Principles

2. Any worker who, acting individually or jointly with other workers, considers that he has grounds for a grievance should have the right –

(a) to submit such grievance without suffering any prejudice whatsoever as a result; and

(b) to have such grievance examined pursuant to an appropriate procedure.

3. The grounds for a grievance may be any measure or situation which concerns the relations between employer and worker or which affects or may affect the conditions of employment of one or several workers in the undertaking when that measure or situation appears contrary to provisions of an applicable collective agreement or of an individual contract of employment, to works rules, to laws or regulations or to the custom or usage of the occupation, branch of economic activity or country, regard being had to principles of good faith.

4. (1) The provisions of this Recommendation are not applicable to collective claims aimed at the modification of terms and conditions of employment.

(2) The determination of the distinction between cases in which a complaint submitted by one or more workers is a grievance to be examined under the procedures provided for in this Recommendation and cases in which a complaint is a general claim to be dealt with by means of collective bargaining or under some other procedure for settlement of disputes is a matter for national law or practice.

5. When procedures for the examination of grievances are established through collective agreements, the parties to such an agreement should be encouraged to include therein a provision to the effect that, during the period of its validity, they undertake to promote settlement of grievances under the procedures provided and to abstain from any action which might impede the effective functioning of these procedures.

6. Workers' organizations or the representatives of the workers in the undertaking should be associated, with equal rights and responsibilities, with the employers or their organizations, preferably by way of agreement, in the establishment and implementation of grievance procedures within the undertaking, in conformity with national law or practice.

7. (1) With a view to minimizing the number of grievances, the greatest attention should be given to the establishment and proper functioning of a sound personnel policy, which should take into account and respect the rights and interests of the workers.

(2) In order to achieve such a policy and to solve social questions affecting the workers within the undertaking, management should, before taking a decision, cooperate with the workers' representatives.

8. As far as possible, grievances should be settled within the undertaking itself according to effective procedures which are adapted to the conditions of the country, branch of economic activity and undertaking concerned and which give the parties concerned every assurance of objectivity.

9. None of the provisions of this Recommendation should result in limiting the right of a worker to apply directly to the competent labour authority or to a labour court or other judicial authority in respect of a grievance, where such right is recognized under national laws or regulations.

III. Procedures within the Undertaking

10. (1) As a general rule an attempt should initially be made to settle grievances directly between the worker affected, whether assisted or not, and his immediate supervisor.

(2) Where such attempt at settlement has failed or where the grievance is of such a nature that a direct discussion between the worker affected and his immediate supervisor would not be appropriate, the worker should be entitled to have his case considered at one or more higher steps, depending on the nature of the grievance and on the structure and size of the undertaking.

11. Grievance procedures should be so formulated and applied that there is a real possibility of achieving at each step provided for by the procedure a settlement of the case freely accepted by the worker and the employer.

12. Grievance procedures should be as uncomplicated and as rapid as possible, and appropriate time limits may be prescribed if necessary for this purpose; formality in the application of these procedures should be kept to a minimum.

13. (1) The worker concerned should have the right to participate directly in the grievance procedure and to be assisted or represented during the examinations of his grievance by a representative of a workers' organization, by a representative of the workers in the undertaking, or by any other person of his own choosing, in conformity with national law or practice.

(2) The employer should have the right to be assisted or represented by an employers' organization.

(3) Any person employed in the same undertaking who assists or represents the worker during the examination of his grievance should, on condition that he acts in conformity with the grievance procedure, enjoy the same protection as that enjoyed by the worker under Paragraph 2, clause (a), of this Recommendation.

14. The worker concerned, or his representative if the latter is employed in the same undertaking, should be allowed sufficient time to participate in the procedure for the examination of the grievance and should not suffer any loss of remuneration because of his absence from work as a result of such participation, account being taken of any rules and practices, including safeguards against abuses, which might be provided for by legislation, collective agreements or other appropriate means.

15. If the parties consider it necessary, minutes of the proceedings may be drawn up in mutual agreement and be available to the parties.

16. (1) Appropriate measures should be taken to ensure that grievance procedures, as well as the rules and practices governing their operation and the conditions for having recourse to them, are brought to the knowledge of the workers.

(2) Any worker who has submitted a grievance should be kept informed of the steps being taken under the procedure and of the action taken on his grievance.

IV. Adjustment of Unsettled Grievances

17. Where all efforts to settle the grievance within the undertaking have failed, there should be a possibility, account being taken of the nature of the grievance, for final settlement of such grievance through one or more of the following procedures:

(a) procedures provided for by collective agreement, such as joint examination of the case by the employers' and workers' organizations concerned or voluntary arbitration by a person or persons designated with the agreement of the employer and worker concerned or their respective organizations;

(b) conciliation or arbitration by the competent public authorities;

(c) recourse to a labour court or other judicial authority;

(d) any other procedure which may be appropriate under national conditions.

18. (1) The worker should be allowed the time off necessary to take part in the procedures referred to in Paragraph 17 of this Recommendation.

(2) Recourse by the worker to any of the procedures provided for in Paragraph 17 should not involve for him any loss of remuneration when his grievance is proved justified in the course of these procedures. Every effort should be made, where possible, for the operation of these procedures outside the working hours of the workers concerned.

www.ingramcontent.com/pod-product-compliance
Ingram Content Group UK Ltd.
Pitfield, Milton Keynes, MK11 3LW, UK
UKHW041849190726
13854UKWH00002B/791

9 789221 108764